Flipping Frier
A Gymnastics Story of Teamwork and Trust

By
KANWAL

COPYRIGHT NOTICE:
All Rights Reserved. This book or any portion thereof may not be reproduced or used in any manner whatsoever without the express written permission of its publisher.

TABLE OF CONTENT

INTRODUCTION 4

Chapter 1: First Day Flips and Wobbles 6

Chapter 2: A Gymnast's Strength 12

Chapter 3: The Fear of Flipping 18

Chapter 4: Confidence Takes a Fall 23

Chapter 5: The Sleepover Pep Talk 30

Chapter 6: Progress and Setbacks 34

Chapter 7: A Lesson from Coach Emma 41

Chapter 8: The Bright Stars Showcase 46

Chapter 9: The Real Victory 51

Chapter 10: What Comes Next? 55

INTRODUCTION

Mia Thompson and Sophie Carter have been best friends for as long as they can remember. They do everything together—ride bikes, play at recess, and now, they're starting something brand new: gymnastics. When they sign up for their first-ever class at Bright Stars Gymnastics Academy, they can't wait to learn how to flip, tumble, and soar through the air like the gymnasts they've watched on TV.

But from the very first practice, they realize that gymnastics isn't as easy as it looks.

Mia is careful and precise, excelling on the balance beam, where control and focus are key. But when it comes to flipping, she freezes. The idea of throwing herself upside-down terrifies her.

Sophie, on the other hand, is fearless. She takes to tumbling like a pro, flipping and leaping across the floor with boundless energy. But there's one problem—her balance is all over the place, and every time she steps onto the beam, she wobbles like she's standing on a tightrope.

As the Bright Stars Showcase approaches, the best friends make a pact—Mia will conquer her fear of flipping, and Sophie will master the balance beam. They'll train together, support each other, and prove that they are stronger as a team.

But as challenges arise and self-doubt creeps in, their friendship is put to the test. Can they push through their fears and achieve their goals? Or will their differences pull them apart?

Flipping Friendship: A Gymnastics Story of Teamwork and Trust is a heartwarming tale about perseverance, confidence, and the power of believing in yourself—and your friends.

Because in gymnastics—and in life—falling isn't failing… as long as you get back up.

Chapter 1: First Day Flips and Wobbles

Mia bounced excitedly on the balls of her feet, gripping the straps of her brand-new gymnastics bag. The smell of fresh chalk and rubber mats filled the air as she and Sophie stepped into Bright Stars Gymnastics Academy for their first real class. The high ceilings stretched above them, crisscrossed with beams and ropes, while the polished spring floor gleamed under the bright lights.

"Whoa," Sophie breathed, spinning in a slow circle to take everything in. "This place is huge!"

Mia nodded, her stomach fluttering—not just from excitement, but from nervousness. She had watched countless gymnastics videos online and practiced cartwheels in her backyard, but this was different. This was real gymnastics, with a real coach and real teammates.

"You girls here for Level One Gymnastics?" came a warm voice.

They turned to see Coach Emma, a tall woman with a confident stance, her blonde hair pulled into a tight bun. She wore a blue tracksuit with the Bright Stars logo and had a kind but focused look in her eyes.

"Yes!" Sophie grinned, practically bouncing in place. "We're so excited!"

"Good to hear," Coach Emma said. "We love excitement here—but we also love hard work. Gymnastics takes patience, practice, and a lot of falling. Think you're up for it?"

Mia swallowed her nerves and nodded determinedly. Sophie, of course, answered with an enthusiastic "Yes!"

Coach Emma led them to the main gym area where a group of girls was already warming up. There were colorful mats, a foam pit, the vault, and the balance beams lined up along the side. A few gymnasts from older classes were practicing back handsprings and cartwheels on the beam, making it look effortless.

Mia's stomach tightened. She barely knew how to do a proper handstand. What if she messed up?

"Alright, everyone!" Coach Emma clapped her hands. "Welcome to Level One Gymnastics. We're going to start with warm-ups, then we'll go over the four main events—vault, bars, beam, and floor. Today is about trying everything so I can see what you're good at and what you need to work on. Sound good?"

A chorus of excited yeses filled the air.

Warm-Up Worries

The group started with stretches—toe touches, lunges, and backbends. Mia and Sophie stuck together, giggling when they wobbled trying to hold their balance on one leg.

Then came jumps—straight jumps, tuck jumps, and split jumps. Sophie soared into the air, her legs almost making a perfect split.

"Nice height, Sophie!" Coach Emma praised.

Mia tried her best, but her jumps weren't as high.

Finally, they moved on to handstands and cartwheels. Sophie eagerly threw herself into a cartwheel, landing with a tiny stumble.

Mia took a deep breath and carefully placed her hands on the mat. She kicked her legs over—except they barely left the ground.

"That's okay, Mia," Coach Emma encouraged. "We'll work on getting those legs higher. You have good form!"

Mia blushed, feeling like everyone was watching her struggle.

"That was great!" Sophie whispered, nudging her. "We'll practice together. You'll be flipping in no time!"

Mia nodded, grateful for her best friend's encouragement.

First Tries on the Equipment

After warm-ups, the real fun began.

Vault came first. They had to run, jump on a springboard, and land with their feet together. Sophie ran full speed, bounced off the board, and landed with a dramatic "Ta-da!"

Mia took a deep breath and ran forward, but when she jumped, she barely made it onto the mat.

"You need more power in your run," Coach Emma told her. "Don't be afraid to go for it!"

Mia nodded, though she still felt uncertain.

Next came bars. They practiced hanging from the bar, swinging their legs, and trying a pull-over, where they lifted their legs over the bar. Mia barely got hers off the ground. Sophie swung easily, laughing when she accidentally spun around too fast.

Balance beam was next. Mia immediately fell in love with it. She carefully walked across, keeping her arms stretched out. She even tried a small jump, landing perfectly.

"Wow, you're really good at this!" Sophie said, clapping.

"You are too!" Mia replied, but Sophie grimaced.

"Not really," she admitted. "The beam is so wobbly. I feel like I'm gonna fall off!"

Mia smiled, relieved that she wasn't the only one struggling with something.

Finally, it was time for floor routines—tumbling, cartwheels, and flips.

"Alright," Coach Emma said. "Who wants to try a round-off?"

Sophie shot her hand up and ran forward confidently. She leaped, twisted her body mid-air, and landed in a near-perfect stance.

The whole class cheered.

"Great energy, Sophie!" Coach Emma said. "A little more control, and that will be perfect."

Mia stared in awe. How did Sophie make it look so easy?

Then it was Mia's turn. Her heart pounded. She ran forward, but at the last second, she froze, landing in a messy cartwheel instead.

She heard a few giggles.

"That's okay, Mia," Coach Emma reassured her. "You'll get there." But Mia couldn't shake the feeling that she was falling behind. The Promise

After practice, the girls sat in the locker room, pulling on their sneakers.

"I can't believe how good you are at tumbling," Mia said.

"And I can't believe how good you are at beam!" Sophie replied. "That thing is terrifying."

Mia sighed. "I wish I could flip like you. But every time I try, I just…freeze."

Sophie thought for a second, then grinned. "How about this? You help me get better on the beam, and I'll help you learn to flip! We'll work together and be the best gymnastics duo ever!"

Mia smiled for the first time all day.

"Deal!" she said, holding out her pinky.

Sophie wrapped her pinky around Mia's, sealing their friendship pact.

Neither of them knew yet just how much they would need each other in the weeks to come.

Chapter 2: A Gymnast's Strength

Mia couldn't stop thinking about gymnastics all week. Every time she closed her eyes, she pictured Sophie flipping effortlessly through the air while she stood frozen on the mat, unable to move.

At school, Sophie wouldn't stop talking about gymnastics either.

"I bet I'll get my back handspring before the showcase," Sophie said at lunch, balancing her apple on her knee like it was a beam.

Mia sighed, poking at her sandwich. "I just hope I can do one flip by then."

"You will!" Sophie said, beaming. "That's what we made our pinky promise for, remember?"

Mia smiled. Sophie's confidence was contagious. Maybe, just maybe, she would learn to flip.

Back at the Gym

When the girls arrived at Bright Stars Gymnastics Academy for their second class, the gym was already buzzing with energy. Some of the older gymnasts were practicing on the high beams, flipping and twisting in the air as if gravity didn't apply to them.

Mia gulped.

Sophie, on the other hand, looked thrilled. "One day, that's gonna be us!" she said, pointing to a girl who had just done a perfect backflip on the beam.

Mia wasn't so sure.

Coach Emma clapped her hands. "Alright, Level One gymnasts, today we're going to work on strength and control. Gymnastics isn't just about being fast or fearless—it's about building muscles, balance, and confidence."

Mia felt a flicker of hope. Maybe she wasn't behind after all.

Strength Training Begins

Coach Emma led them through a series of strength drills—push-ups, hollow body holds, leg lifts.

Mia struggled at first, but she quickly realized something amazing—she was actually pretty strong. Her balance beam training made her core muscles steady, and she could hold a hollow body position longer than most of the other girls.

Sophie, however, was already getting impatient.

"Ugh," she groaned, flopping onto her back after her third attempt at push-ups. "Why do we need to do all this? I just wanna flip!"

"Because," Coach Emma said, kneeling beside her, "flipping isn't just about jumping. It's about control. If you don't have strength, you won't be able to land safely."

Sophie pouted but got back up.

Mia smiled to herself. Maybe for once, she had the advantage.

The Friendly Rivalry Begins

After strength training, the class split into small groups to practice different skills.

Sophie and Mia ended up with Jasmine, the most competitive girl in their class. Jasmine had been doing gymnastics longer than everyone else and always acted like she was the best.

"Let's see how good you guys really are," Jasmine said, flipping her sleek ponytail over her shoulder.

Sophie's eyes narrowed playfully. "Oh, it's on."

The three girls started taking turns at different challenges.

First up: cartwheels.

Jasmine's were nearly perfect—legs straight, arms strong, toes pointed.

Sophie's were energetic but slightly messy, and Mia's… well, she was still working on getting her legs up all the way.

"Not bad," Jasmine said, looking at Sophie. Then she glanced at Mia and smirked. "You just need to actually get off the ground."

Mia's face burned.

Next was balance beam.

Mia's confidence soared as she stepped onto the beam. She glided across it with ease, finishing with a small jump at the end.

Jasmine nodded approvingly. "Okay, you're good at beam."

Sophie wobbled across the beam, nearly falling off twice before she made it to the end.

Jasmine laughed. "Wow, Sophie, you look like a flamingo on roller skates."

Sophie grinned. "Hey, at least I can flip! Let's see you do that, Miss Perfect."

Coach Emma called them over to the floor mats for tumbling practice.

Jasmine went first. She did a beautiful round-off, landing with a dramatic pose.

Sophie followed, springing into the air and landing a fast, if slightly crooked, round-off.

Then it was Mia's turn. Her stomach twisted.

She ran forward, but as she reached the spot where she needed to push off, her feet stopped moving. Instead of flipping, she just froze, standing awkwardly in place.

Jasmine laughed. "That was the worst round-off I've ever seen."

Mia felt like melting into the mat.

Sophie jumped in immediately. "Hey! At least she's trying."

Jasmine shrugged. "If she's too scared to flip, maybe gymnastics isn't for her."

Tears pricked Mia's eyes, but she refused to let them fall.

Coach Emma must have noticed, because she walked over and said, "Gymnastics isn't about being fearless. It's about facing your fears and pushing through them. Mia, we'll work on this together. You'll get there."

Mia nodded, though doubt still weighed heavily on her shoulders.

A New Challenge

As class wrapped up, Sophie pulled Mia aside.

"Forget Jasmine," Sophie said. "She's just being mean because she wants to be the best at everything."

Mia nodded, but she still felt frustrated with herself. "I just wish I wasn't so scared."

Sophie tapped her chin, thinking. Then she snapped her fingers.

"I got it! Let's make a new challenge," she said. "I'll help you with flips, and you help me with the balance beam. We'll train together until the showcase."

Mia hesitated. "What if I never get it?"

Sophie grabbed her hands. "You will. You just need to keep trying."

Mia took a deep breath. Maybe Sophie was right. Maybe all she needed was time—and a really good training partner.

"Okay," Mia said, determined now. "Let's do it."

Sophie grinned. "Best gymnastics duo ever?"

Mia held out her pinky. "Best gymnastics duo ever."

They linked pinkies, sealing their deal.

Neither of them knew just how much their challenge would test their friendship in the weeks to come.

Chapter 3: The Fear of Flipping

Mia's legs trembled as she stood at the edge of the spring floor, staring at the blue mat in front of her.

"Okay, Mia," Coach Emma said, kneeling beside her. "You don't have to flip all the way yet. Just work on your round-off. One step at a time."

Mia took a deep breath and nodded. One step at a time.

She ran forward, placed her hands on the mat, and kicked her legs over—except she barely left the ground. Her landing was clumsy, her legs uneven, and she wobbled before standing straight.

"That's okay," Coach Emma encouraged. "Try again."

Mia tried three more times, but each attempt felt worse than the last.

Across the gym, Sophie was laughing and flipping with ease.

"Nice, Sophie!" Coach Emma called as Sophie landed a perfect front handspring.

Mia's stomach twisted. Sophie made flipping look so easy. Why couldn't she do it?

Different Strengths, Different Struggles
After practice, Mia and Sophie sat on the bleachers, sipping water.

"I can't do it," Mia mumbled, staring at the floor.

"Yes, you can," Sophie insisted. "You just have to stop thinking so much and just go for it!"

Mia frowned. "That's easy for you to say. You're fearless."

Sophie sighed. "Well, I wish I had your balance skills. I still feel like I'm going to fall off the beam every time I step on it."

Mia looked up. "Really?"

Sophie nodded. "Yesterday, I tried a leap, and I almost crashed into the judges' table."

Mia giggled at the thought. "That bad?"

"That bad," Sophie said dramatically. "So… I'll help you flip, and you help me survive the beam?"

Mia smiled. "Deal."

The First Flip Attempt

That afternoon, Mia and Sophie practiced in Mia's backyard.

Mia's mom had laid out a soft mat on the grass for them. "Just in case someone gets too daring," she had joked, looking at Sophie.

Sophie rolled her eyes playfully. "Moms worry too much."

Mia, however, was grateful for the extra padding.

"Okay," Sophie said, standing on the mat. "First, let's try a handstand. If you want to flip, you have to get comfortable going upside-down."

Mia groaned. "I hate handstands."

"You'll love them by the end of today!" Sophie declared.

She demonstrated a perfect handstand, legs straight, toes pointed. "See? Easy."

Mia gulped and tried one. She kicked up but barely got her legs above her waist before falling sideways.

Sophie laughed. "Okay, not bad, but let's try again. This time, kick harder!"

Mia tried again. And again. And again. Each time, she either wobbled, fell, or didn't kick high enough.

After ten attempts, she flopped onto the mat in frustration.

"This is hopeless," Mia groaned.

Sophie sat down next to her. "No, it's not! You're getting better. You just need to trust yourself."

Mia sighed. "What if I never get it?"

Sophie grinned. "Then I'll just carry you through the air during our routine."

Mia burst out laughing. "I'd like to see you try."

Sophie's Turn to Struggle

The next day at gymnastics practice, Sophie had to face her own fears.

"Alright, Sophie," Coach Emma said as she stood beside the balance beam. "Today, I want you to try a leap."

Sophie gulped. She had been avoiding jumps on the beam because they terrified her.

She stepped up and took a deep breath. I can do this.

She took a few small steps, bent her knees, and leapt—

—And immediately panicked.

Her feet wobbled as she landed. She flailed her arms to keep from falling—but it was too late. She slipped off the side and landed on the mat with a thud.

A few girls giggled. Jasmine smirked. "Yikes. That was rough."

Sophie's cheeks burned red. She wanted to act like she didn't care, but inside, she felt just as embarrassed as Mia had felt about her flips.

Mia hurried over and helped Sophie stand. "You okay?"

Sophie nodded, but her confidence had cracked.

Coach Emma smiled reassuringly. "You need to slow down and focus on your landing. You'll get it, Sophie."

Sophie didn't feel so sure anymore.

A Shift in Confidence

After practice, the girls sat on the locker room bench.

"I think I'm cursed," Sophie muttered.

Mia raised an eyebrow. "Cursed?"

"Yeah. Some gymnasts are just meant to be tumblers. And some are meant to be beam queens, like you."

Mia shook her head. "You're not cursed. You just need more practice."

Sophie sighed. "Maybe."

"Maybe?" Mia smirked. "Or definitely?"

Sophie rolled her eyes, but a small smile tugged at her lips. "Fine. Definitely."

Mia grinned. "Good. Because tomorrow, we're conquering the beam together."

The Deal Becomes a Real Challenge

That night, Mia and Sophie texted each other.

Sophie: Okay, here's the deal. You do one flip attempt every day. I do one beam jump every day. No excuses.

Mia: Ugh. Fine. But you have to promise you won't quit when you fall off the beam again.

Sophie: Same to you about flipping!

Mia: Deal.

They both sent pinky promise emojis.

Neither of them realized just how tough this challenge would become.

Chapter 4: Confidence Takes a Fall

Sophie stood at the edge of the balance beam, her arms stretched out for balance.

She took a deep breath, trying to push away the nerves buzzing in her stomach.

You can do this, she told herself.

One small leap. That's all she had to do.

She bent her knees, pushed off the beam, and—WOBBLE.

Her landing was shaky. Her ankle tilted too far, and before she could stop herself—THUD.

She hit the mat hard.

Lying on her back, she let out a groan.

"That was worse than last time," she muttered.

Coach Emma walked over and held out a hand. "Not worse," she said. "Just another attempt."

Sophie let Coach Emma help her up, but her frustration only grew.

She had promised Mia that she would conquer the beam, but no matter how hard she tried, she couldn't land one simple jump without nearly crashing to the floor.

Mia's Turn to Struggle

On the other side of the gym, Mia was staring at the floor mat, her hands clenched into fists.

"Alright, Mia," Coach Emma said gently. "Let's try a small flip—just a little hop over. I'll spot you."

Mia's stomach twisted. She didn't want to try. But she had promised Sophie.

Taking a deep breath, she ran forward, placed her hands on the mat, kicked her legs over—

—And stopped halfway.

Instead of flipping, her legs froze in the air, and she came crashing down onto her back.

The wind rushed out of her lungs.

The moment she hit the ground, laughter erupted from the other side of the gym.

Mia turned her head and saw Jasmine smirking.

"Wow," Jasmine said. "That was the slowest flip I've ever seen."

Mia's cheeks burned.

Coach Emma helped her sit up. "You hesitated," she said. "Your body wanted to go, but your mind held you back."

Mia nodded, swallowing the lump in her throat.

She was so tired of failing.

A Growing Frustration

That evening, Mia and Sophie sat outside on Mia's backyard trampoline, their moods gloomy.

"Today was the worst," Mia muttered.

Sophie sighed. "Tell me about it."

"I keep freezing every time I try to flip," Mia said, bouncing lightly on the trampoline.

"And I keep falling off the beam like a total disaster," Sophie groaned, flopping onto her back. "I just don't get it! I can flip on the floor, but I feel like a baby giraffe on the beam!"

Mia sighed. "Maybe Jasmine's right. Maybe I'm not meant to flip."

Sophie sat up quickly. "Don't say that. If I'm not allowed to quit, you're not allowed to quit either."

Mia gave her a half-smile. "Fine. But only if you promise not to quit either."

Sophie smirked. "Deal."

They linked pinkies, but for the first time, doubt lingered between them.

The Next Day—And A Big Mistake

The next day at practice, tensions were high.

Mia was determined to flip. She had to.

Sophie was determined to land her beam routine. She had to.

When it was time for floor practice, Mia took a deep breath and charged forward, ready to flip—

But she hesitated again.

Instead of flipping over, she stopped halfway, her hands slipping out from under her.

She landed on her side, pain shooting up her arm.

Coach Emma rushed over. "Mia! Are you okay?"

Mia nodded, though her arm ached.

Jasmine shook her head. "You just need to commit," she said. "Or don't bother trying."

Mia's chest burned with embarrassment.

She turned to Sophie, expecting her usual encouragement But Sophie was staring at the beam, lost in her own frustration.

And then—she made a mistake.

Sophie climbed onto the beam, angry and impatient, and tried to leap again

But she rushed it. She jumped too fast, didn't land straight—And slipped. CRASH.

Sophie hit the mat hard, her arm twisting awkwardly beneath her.

A sharp gasp spread through the gym.

Mia jumped up. "Sophie!"

Coach Emma was already kneeling beside her. "Don't move yet," she said gently. "Let me check your arm."

Tears welled in Sophie's eyes. "I—I think I landed wrong."

Mia's stomach twisted with guilt. This was her fault.

They had been so focused on their challenge that Sophie had pushed herself too hard.

At the Doctor's Office

A few hours later, Mia sat in the waiting room at the doctor's office, nervously tapping her foot.

Sophie's mom had taken her to get her arm checked, and Mia had begged her mom to let her come along.

Finally, Sophie walked out, her arm wrapped in a blue brace.

Mia's heart sank.

Sophie flopped into the chair beside her. "Well," she sighed, "it's not broken. Just a sprain."

Mia exhaled in relief. "Thank goodness."

"But I have to rest it for a whole week," Sophie groaned. "No gymnastics."

Mia bit her lip. "I'm sorry," she whispered.

Sophie frowned. "Why are you sorry?"

"Because…" Mia hesitated. "We were pushing each other so hard. I should have told you to slow down."

Sophie was quiet for a moment. Then she smiled weakly. "Yeah… maybe we both went a little overboard."

Mia looked at her. "So… does this mean we're done with our challenge?"

Sophie grinned. "Are you kidding? No way."

Mia's eyes widened. "But—"

"Listen," Sophie said. "I'll take a break, but as soon as my arm's better, we're back to training. You're still learning to flip, and I still have to beat that stupid beam."

Mia couldn't help but laugh. "Okay, fine. But no more getting hurt."

Sophie smirked. "Same to you, Miss Hesitates-to-Flip."

Mia rolled her eyes. "You'll see. One day, I'll flip perfectly."

Sophie nudged her. "And I'll land a perfect beam routine."

Mia smiled. "Deal."

They bumped fists—a new promise.

This time, though, they knew they had to train smarter, not harder.

Chapter 5: The Sleepover Pep Talk

Sophie hated sitting still.

For the past three days, she had been forced to rest her arm, and she was miserable. No cartwheels. No flips. No beam (not that she missed it).

Worst of all? No gymnastics practice.

Mia had gone to practice without her, and though she sent updates through text—Jasmine is still annoying, I actually did a straight handstand today!—Sophie felt like she was missing out on everything.

So when Mia invited her over for a sleepover, Sophie jumped at the chance. If she couldn't train, at least she could talk about gymnastics all night.

The Sleepover Begins

Sophie arrived at Mia's house with her sleeping bag, a bag of gummy bears, and her gymnastics notebook.

Mia's mom ordered pizza, and they set up a makeshift fort in the living room with blankets and pillows.

They settled in with slices of pepperoni pizza and opened Sophie's notebook, where she had sketched out gymnastics moves and written little notes to herself.

Mia pointed to one. "Beat the beam, no fear" was written in big, bold letters.

Sophie groaned. "Ugh. My own handwriting is mocking me."

Mia grinned. "Well, you'll be back on the beam soon. And I will flip before the showcase."

Sophie raised an eyebrow. "Wait. Did you actually try again?"

Mia hesitated, then sighed. "Kind of. Coach Emma spotted me today. I got my legs over, but I still landed badly."

Sophie sat up straighter. "That's progress! You actually flipped!"

Mia shrugged. "Sort of. I still felt like I was falling. Like my body didn't trust me to land right."

Sophie thought for a moment. "You know, when I was little, I was scared of the monkey bars."

Mia blinked. "You? Scared of something?"

Sophie nodded. "I was terrified. I thought if I let go, I'd fall and break my arm. But then my brother told me something."

"What?"

Sophie grinned. "He said, 'You're going to fall anyway. Might as well do it like a gymnast.'"

Mia stared at her. "What does that even mean?"

"It means," Sophie said dramatically, "that falling is part of learning. So instead of being scared of it, you just have to fall the right way and get back up."

Mia thought about that. Maybe flipping wasn't about avoiding the fall. Maybe it was about learning to land.

The Movie That Changed Everything

After dinner, they curled up with a gymnastics movie—a classic about a young gymnast who overcame fear to win a big competition.

Mia watched as the girl in the movie struggled with her back handspring. She failed over and over again—falling, stumbling, almost giving up.

But then, after weeks of practice, she finally landed it.

Mia's stomach fluttered.

Maybe that could be her.

Sophie nudged her. "Thinking what I'm thinking?"

Mia grinned. "That I'm going to be flipping nonstop at practice tomorrow?"

Sophie smirked. "Now that's the spirit."

Training Smarter, Not Harder

The next day at practice, Sophie sat on the bleachers, forced to watch instead of train.

It was torture.

But when Coach Emma announced floor practice, Sophie sat up straighter. This was Mia's moment.

Mia took her spot on the mat, rolling her shoulders. Her heart pounded, but she kept Sophie's words in her head.

"You're going to fall anyway. Might as well do it like a gymnast."

She took a deep breath. Ran forward. Kicked off.

And SHE FLIPPED.

She landed on her feet, though she stumbled slightly.

A burst of excitement filled her chest. She had done it!

Sophie leaped off the bleachers, ignoring her sore arm. "MIA! YOU DID IT!!"

Mia beamed, feeling lighter than ever.

Jasmine raised an eyebrow. "Huh. Not bad."

Coach Emma clapped. "That was your best attempt yet. Now, let's clean up that landing."

Mia grinned. She wasn't scared anymore.

Sophie cheered from the sidelines. She couldn't train yet, but she knew—soon, it would be her turn to conquer the beam.

Chapter 6: Progress and Setbacks

Sophie bounced on her toes, itching to get back onto the floor. One whole week without training had been pure torture. She was finally cleared to return—but her wrist still felt a little stiff.

Mia, standing beside her, grinned excitedly. "Are you ready?"

Sophie smirked. "Obviously. I've been dreaming about getting back in here. I'm going to destroy that beam."

Mia nodded. "And I'm going to land my flip without stumbling."

The best friends fist-bumped.

They had one week left before the Bright Stars Showcase, and they were ready to prove themselves.

Mia's Biggest Challenge Yet

Warm-ups went smoothly. Mia nailed her cartwheels, held her handstand for five seconds, and stuck her round-off perfectly.

When it was time for floor practice, she took a deep breath and lined up for her flip.

No more fear, she told herself.

She ran, pushed off the ground, flipped—

—And landed cleanly.

Her knees bent slightly, but she didn't stumble.

Sophie jumped up and down. "YES! That was PERFECT!"

Coach Emma smiled. "Great work, Mia! That's exactly what I wanted to see. Now…" She paused. "Are you ready for something new?"

Mia froze. "New?"

Coach Emma nodded. "You've been working on front handsprings. I think you're ready to try a back handspring."

Mia's stomach flipped harder than she ever had.

A back handspring? That meant jumping backward.

Suddenly, all her fear came rushing back.

Sophie's Return to the Beam

While Mia tried to wrap her mind around back handsprings, Sophie faced her own battle.

She stood in front of the balance beam, her arms stiff at her sides.

She'd fallen before. She'd gotten hurt before.

What if I fall again?

Mia ran up beside her. "You got this!"

Sophie took a deep breath and stepped onto the beam.

One foot forward. Then another.

Easy. She could walk on the beam just fine.

Coach Emma called out, "Okay, Sophie. Let's try a leap."

Sophie's hands felt sweaty. Her heartbeat pounded in her ears.

She bent her knees, pushed off—

And froze midair.

Her feet barely left the beam, and instead of a smooth landing, she wobbled wildly, her arms flailing.

She tried to steady herself, but her balance was already gone. THUD. Sophie hit the mat hard, just like before.

The whole gym went silent.

Jasmine muttered, "Not again…"

Sophie sat up slowly, her face burning red.

Mia rushed over. "Are you okay?"

Sophie felt fine physically, but her confidence was shattered.

She got up, dusting herself off. "I—I'm fine," she mumbled.

Coach Emma studied her closely. "Sophie, I want you to take a deep breath."

Sophie inhaled shakily.

"You're hesitating because you don't trust yourself," Coach Emma said. "You're thinking about falling, instead of thinking about the landing."

Sophie nodded, but inside, she felt horrible.

She was supposed to be fearless.

She wasn't supposed to be scared.

Doubt and Frustration

After practice, Mia and Sophie sat outside the gym, sipping their water bottles.

Mia frowned. "Sophie, you're usually so confident. What's going on?"

Sophie stared at the ground. "I don't know. Ever since I fell, I just… I can't do it. I feel like I'm going to mess up every time."

Mia hesitated, then admitted, "That's how I felt about flipping."

Sophie sighed. "Yeah, but you overcame it. You're flipping now."

Mia nudged her. "And you'll beat the beam. You just need more time."

Sophie wasn't so sure.

The showcase was only a few days away, and she couldn't even land a basic leap.

What if she embarrassed herself?

What if she let everyone down?

What if she just wasn't good enough?

Mia suddenly stood up. "Come on."

Sophie frowned. "Where?"

Mia grinned. "You helped me practice flipping at my house. Now it's my turn to help you."

Sophie hesitated. "Mia, I don't think—"

Mia grabbed her hand. "Trust me."

Sophie took a deep breath.

Mia trusted me when she was scared. I can trust her now.

"Okay," she said. "Let's do this."

Training Under the Stars

That night, Mia and Sophie set up a mini balance beam on the grass in Mia's backyard. It wasn't as high as the real thing, but it was enough to practice safely.

Mia placed a hand on Sophie's shoulder. "We're going to take this slow. No pressure, no rushing."

Sophie nodded, feeling a little better.

She stepped onto the beam.

Mia stood beside her, holding out her arms for support. "Okay, just walk across first."

Sophie walked, her steps steadier than earlier.

Mia smiled. "Now try a little jump."

Sophie bent her knees and jumped the tiniest bit, barely lifting off the beam.

Mia laughed. "Come on, you can jump higher than that!"

Sophie smiled for the first time all day.

She tried again—this time, lifting her feet higher.

She landed cleanly.

Mia clapped. "Yes! That's it!"

Sophie felt a spark of confidence return.

Maybe she wasn't hopeless after all.

A Renewed Promise

After practicing for an hour, they lay on Mia's trampoline, staring up at the night sky.

Sophie sighed. "I still don't know if I can do it in front of an audience."

Mia turned to her. "Do you remember what you told me?"

Sophie raised an eyebrow. "I tell you a lot of things."

Mia grinned. "You said, 'You're going to fall anyway. Might as well do it like a gymnast.'"

Sophie laughed. "I did say that, didn't I?"

Mia sat up. "You'll land your beam routine. Maybe not tomorrow. Maybe not at the showcase. But you will get there."

Sophie smiled. "And you'll land a perfect back handspring."

Mia groaned. "Ugh. Let's just focus on one thing at a time."

They laughed, but deep down, Sophie felt hopeful again. She still had a lot to work on, but for the first time in days, she felt ready to try again.

Chapter 7: A Lesson from Coach Emma

The Bright Stars Showcase was only two days away, and the entire gym buzzed with nervous energy.

Mia and Sophie stood side by side, watching the older gymnasts rehearse their routines. They made everything look so effortless—flipping high into the air, landing gracefully, sticking their dismounts without a wobble.

Mia gulped.

Sophie shifted uncomfortably.

The pressure was starting to feel real.

Coach Emma clapped her hands. "Alright, Level One gymnasts, today is our final practice before the showcase. This is your chance to work through your routines and fix any last details. Remember—it's not about perfection. It's about confidence and control."

Mia took a deep breath. Confidence and control. I can do that. Right?

Sophie wasn't so sure.

Mia's Back Handspring Attempt

When it was time for floor practice, Mia stood at the edge of the mat, staring at the spot where she needed to jump.

She had landed her front handspring perfectly yesterday, but back handsprings were a different story.

Her brain screamed, "Don't go backward!" every time she tried.

Coach Emma stood beside her. "You've got this, Mia. I'll spot you."

Mia took a deep breath, bent her knees, and—

Stopped.

Her body froze.

Sophie, watching from the side, chewed her lip. She had seen this same hesitation over and over again.

"You're overthinking it," Coach Emma said gently. "Trust yourself."

Mia tried again.

She jumped backward—barely.

Coach Emma caught her, but Mia collapsed onto her knees.

She groaned in frustration. "Why can't I just do it?"

Coach Emma knelt beside her. "Do you know what gymnastics is really about?"

Mia frowned. "Flipping?"

Coach Emma smiled. "It's about trusting yourself. It's about knowing that even if you fall, you have the strength to get back up."

Mia exhaled. Maybe she wasn't trusting herself enough.

Maybe she needed to stop fighting the fall and just go for it.

Sophie's Final Beam Test

While Mia battled her back handspring, Sophie faced her own worst enemy—the balance beam.

Coach Emma called her name.

Sophie hesitated.

Her heart pounded as she stepped up.

What if I fall again?

Coach Emma gave her a knowing look. "Sophie, gymnastics isn't about never falling. It's about knowing how to get back up."

Sophie took a deep breath.

She walked across the beam. Steady. Strong.

She bent her knees.

And then—

She jumped.

For a split second, she felt weightless.

And then—she landed.

She wobbled.

But she didn't fall.

Mia cheered. "SOPHIE! YOU DID IT!"

Coach Emma smiled. "See? You had it in you all along."

Sophie grinned. Maybe she wasn't perfect yet, but for the first time in weeks, she felt like a real gymnast again.

A Private Moment of Doubt

After practice, Mia and Sophie sat on the benches, finishing their water.

"I still don't know if I can do the back handspring at the showcase," Mia admitted.

Sophie nudged her. "You don't have to. Just do what you feel ready for."

Mia sighed. "But if I don't do it, I'll feel like I failed."

Sophie frowned. "Mia… you already won."

Mia blinked. "What do you mean?"

Sophie smiled. "A few weeks ago, you couldn't even do a flip. Now, you're landing handsprings. That's a win."

Mia thought about that. Maybe Sophie was right.

She wasn't perfect yet.

But she was better than she had been before.

And maybe… that was enough.

The Night Before the Showcase

That night, Mia tossed and turned in bed.

She kept picturing herself at the showcase—standing in front of all those people.

Would she freeze? Would she mess up?

She rolled onto her back, staring at the ceiling.

Then she whispered, "I can do this."

She wasn't just saying it.

She was starting to believe it.

Chapter 8: The Bright Stars Showcase

The gym was buzzing with excitement.

Rows of folding chairs lined the floor, filled with parents, siblings, and friends. Judges sat at a long table, clipboards in hand. Colorful banners hung from the rafters, and the scent of fresh chalk and rubber mats filled the air.

Mia's heart thudded in her chest as she peeked through the curtain behind the competition floor.

"This is it," she whispered.

Sophie stood beside her, adjusting her sparkly purple leotard. "Are you ready?"

Mia wasn't sure.

She had practiced for weeks. She had overcome so much fear.

But standing here, in front of so many people, she felt like she was back at square one.

Nerves and Butterflies

The Level One gymnasts lined up, waiting for their names to be called.

Mia wiped her sweaty palms on her leotard.

Sophie bounced in place. "I feel like I'm going to explode."

Mia forced a smile. "Excited?"

"Nervous," Sophie admitted. "But mostly excited."

Coach Emma knelt beside them. "Remember, girls—this is just a showcase. No scores, no medals. Just you showing what you've learned."

Mia swallowed hard. That should have made her feel better. It didn't.

Sophie grabbed her hand. "We got this."

Mia squeezed back. "Yeah. We got this."

Sophie Faces the Beam—For Real This Time

Sophie's name was called first.

She took a deep breath and walked onto the balance beam.

The crowd was silent.

Sophie climbed up, her heart racing.

Don't fall. Don't fall. Don't fall.

She started her routine.

One foot in front of the other. Smooth. Steady. Controlled.

Then came the leap.

She bent her knees, pushed off the beam—

And landed.

A tiny wobble. But she was still on the beam.

A rush of pure joy filled her chest.

She finished the routine with a small jump dismount, sticking the landing.

The audience clapped and cheered.

Sophie's smile was so wide it hurt.

She did it.

As she walked off the mat, Mia wrapped her in a hug. "I knew you could do it!"

Sophie beamed. "It actually felt… easy."

Mia grinned. "Told you."

Mia's Moment of Truth

Mia's name was called for floor routine.

Her stomach flipped.

She walked onto the spring floor, trying to ignore the hundreds of eyes watching her.

She took her starting pose.

The music began.

She moved through her choreography, landing her jumps smoothly.

Then came the moment she had dreaded.

The tumbling pass.

She had two choices:
- Play it safe with a front handspring.
- Go for it and try the back handspring.

She hesitated for half a second.

Then she thought of Sophie's words.

"You're going to fall anyway. Might as well do it like a gymnast."

She took a deep breath.

And jumped.

For a split second, time slowed.

She felt her body tilt backward, her hands hitting the mat—

Then her feet landed.

She wobbled slightly but didn't fall.

She had done it. A real back handspring.

The crowd erupted in cheers.

Mia's heart soared.

She finished her routine, took her final pose, and ran off the mat grinning so hard her face hurt.

Sophie tackled her in a hug. "MIA. YOU DID A BACK HANDSPRING."

Mia giggled breathlessly. "I KNOW."

Coach Emma ruffled her hair. "I told you—you had it in you all along."

Mia felt unstoppable.

The End of the Showcase

When the showcase ended, all the gymnasts received ribbons and certificates.

Jasmine won first place, but for the first time ever—Mia and Sophie didn't care.

They had won something even bigger.

They had overcome their fears.

They had proved to themselves that they were real gymnasts.

The Next Challenge Awaits

Later that evening, Mia and Sophie sat on Mia's trampoline, staring up at the stars.

"So what now?" Mia asked.

Sophie smirked. "Now? We train for the next competition."

Mia laughed. "What if I don't want to?"

Sophie nudged her. "You're a gymnast now. There's no going back."

Mia smiled. She wouldn't have it any other way.

Chapter 9: The Real Victory

The Bright Stars Showcase was over, but the buzz of excitement still lingered in the gym.

Parents congratulated their kids, teammates huddled together to replay their best moments, and Coach Emma stood at the front, handing out certificates of achievement to each gymnast.

Mia clutched hers tightly, rereading the words:

Mia Thompson – Most Improved Gymnast

A warm sense of pride filled her chest.

She had done it.

Not just the showcase—not just the back handspring—but everything. She had faced her biggest fear, and now she felt like a real gymnast.

Sophie bumped her shoulder. "Well, Miss Most Improved, how does it feel?"

Mia grinned. "Pretty great."

Sophie twirled her ribbon between her fingers. "I still can't believe you went for the back handspring."

Mia laughed. "Me neither."

Coach Emma called out, "Alright, everyone! Before you go celebrate, I want to say something."

The gym quieted as she stepped forward, smiling. "Each of you worked so hard to be here today. It wasn't about who won first place or who had the best routine. It was about showing up, pushing yourselves, and learning. That's what makes you gymnasts—not the medals, not the trophies, but the effort you put in every single day."

Mia and Sophie exchanged a glance.

They knew that better than anyone.

Coach Emma continued, "And for those of you who are ready for a new challenge, we'll be starting training for our first real gymnastics competition next season."

Gasps and whispers spread through the group.

A real competition?

Mia's stomach did a little flip—this time, not from fear, but excitement.

Sophie's eyes lit up. "Mia. We HAVE to do it."

Mia hesitated. "I don't know…"

Sophie grabbed her shoulders. "Listen to me. You literally just did a back handspring in front of a huge crowd. YOU ARE READY."

Mia bit her lip. "What if I'm not?"

Sophie smirked. "Then I'll drag you to practice anyway."

Mia laughed. "Fine. But only if you promise to keep working on beam."

Sophie groaned. "Ugh, fine. You drive a hard bargain."

They shook hands, sealing their next big challenge.

Post-Showcase Celebration

Later that evening, the whole Level One team met up at Pizza Palace for a celebration.

Mia and Sophie shared a large cheese pizza, surrounded by their teammates. Even Jasmine was in a good mood, bragging about her first-place finish—but in a way that didn't sound as mean as usual.

"I have to admit," Jasmine said, twirling her straw in her soda, "your back handspring wasn't bad, Mia."

Mia raised an eyebrow. "Was that a compliment?"

Jasmine smirked. "Don't get used to it."

Sophie snickered. "I think she likes us now."

Mia grinned. "We're growing on her."

As the night went on, Mia felt a new kind of happiness. Not just because of the showcase. Not just because of the gymnastics.

But because of the friends she had made along the way.

A Moment Under the Stars

After the celebration, Sophie and Mia sat on Mia's backyard trampoline, staring up at the night sky.

"So," Sophie said, stretching her arms behind her head, "do you think we'll ever get tired of gymnastics?"

Mia thought about it.

All the times she had struggled. All the times she had wanted to quit.

And yet, she was still here.

Still flipping. Still learning. Still loving every second of it.

Mia smiled. "I don't think so."

Sophie grinned. "Me neither."

They lay there in comfortable silence, the stars twinkling above them, the memories of the showcase still fresh in their minds.

There would be new challenges.

New fears to face. New victories to celebrate.

But one thing was certain:

Whatever happened next, they would face it together.

Chapter 10: What Comes Next?

A week after the Bright Stars Showcase, Mia and Sophie stood side by side at the entrance of Bright Stars Gymnastics Academy, watching the older gymnasts train.

The gym was bustling with energy—the Level Two and Level Three girls were flipping across the floor, swinging on the bars, and tumbling like they belonged in the Olympics.

Sophie let out a low whistle. "That's going to be us soon."

Mia swallowed hard. "You mean... we're really doing this?"

Sophie smirked. "We pinky promised. No backing out now."

Mia took a deep breath. She had promised. And now, it was time for the next big step.

The First Competition Meeting

That afternoon, Coach Emma gathered the Level One girls for an important announcement.

"As you all know, the Bright Stars Showcase was just for fun," she said, smiling. "But this? This is different. You're about to start training for your first real gymnastics competition."

Mia felt her stomach flip.

Sophie bounced excitedly in her seat.

"This means more intense practices, working on perfecting your skills, and, most importantly, competing against other gyms."

The girls gasped. Other gyms?!

Jasmine leaned forward, grinning. "Finally. Some real competition."

Mia gulped. If she thought performing at the showcase was scary, this was a hundred times worse.

Coach Emma continued, "You'll each compete in at least two events—floor, beam, vault, or bars. Some of you may do all four."

Sophie whispered, "You're definitely doing floor."

Mia whispered back, "And you're definitely doing beam."

Sophie groaned dramatically. "Ugh, why did I agree to this?"

Mia smirked. "Because I won't let you quit."

Sophie rolled her eyes but grinned.

Training Gets Real

Over the next few weeks, practice became more intense.

Mia worked on perfecting her back handspring. At first, she still hesitated, but each time she tried, the fear became smaller.

One afternoon, after three solid attempts, Coach Emma clapped her hands.

"Mia, I think you're ready to try a back handspring on your own."

Mia froze. "Wait… what?"

Coach Emma smiled. "You've got the strength, the technique—you just have to believe in yourself."

Mia turned to Sophie.

Sophie gave her a thumbs-up. "You got this."

Mia took a deep breath.

She bent her knees. Pushed off. Flipped backward.

And landed on her feet—without any help.

She stood up, stunned.

Sophie shrieked. "MIA! YOU DID IT!!"

Mia grinned so wide her face hurt. "I DID IT!!"

Coach Emma smiled proudly. "See? I knew you could."

Mia had never felt prouder.

Sophie's Final Battle With the Beam

Meanwhile, Sophie was still at war with the balance beam.

She could do her routine on the low beam perfectly, but the moment she stepped onto the high beam, her confidence wobbled.

One day, after another shaky practice, she plopped onto the mat beside Mia.

"This beam is the worst."

Mia laughed. "You said the same thing about my flips, and now look at me."

Sophie pouted. "Yeah, yeah."

Mia nudged her. "You'll get it. You just have to trust yourself."

Sophie sighed, staring up at the gym ceiling. "You sound like Coach Emma."

Mia smirked. "Maybe I should be a coach someday."

Sophie snorted. "You'd be the most dramatic coach ever."

They both burst out laughing.

A New Goal, A New Promise

That night, they sat on Mia's backyard trampoline, looking up at the stars—just like they always did.

"So," Mia said, "we're really doing this. A real competition."

Sophie grinned. "Yup. And after that? Who knows? Maybe we'll go to the Olympics."

Mia laughed. "One step at a time."

They sat in comfortable silence, thinking about everything they had been through.

The struggles.

The falls.

The victories.

And through it all, they had never given up.

Sophie held out her pinky finger. "One more promise."

Mia linked hers. "What is it?"

"No matter how hard things get… no matter how many times we fall…" Sophie smiled. "We always get back up."

Mia smiled back. "Deal."

Their pinkies locked.

The stars twinkled above them.

And their gymnastics journey?

It was only just beginning.

Printed in Great Britain
by Amazon